T0194863

LEAVING HOME

WITH

PEACE

AND

PURPOSE

MARY A. HIBDON

WESTBOW
PRESS®
A DIVISION OF THOMAS NELSON
& ZONDERVAN

Scriptural passages taken from the Bible Gateway app.

Other Sources

Charles H. Spurgeon, *Morning and Evening: An Updated Edition of the Classical Devotional in Today's Language* (Nashville, TN: Thomas Nelson, Inc., 1994).

My Utmost Devotional Bible (Nashville, TN: Thomas Nelson, Inc., 1982).

WestBow Press books may be ordered through booksellers or by contacting:

WestBow Press
A Division of Thomas Nelson & Zondervan
1663 Liberty Drive
Bloomington, IN 47403
www.westbowpress.com
1 (866) 928-1240

ISBN: 978-1-9736-1065-6 (sc)
ISBN: 978-1-9736-1064-9 (e)

Library of Congress Control Number: 2017918880

Print information available on the last page.

WestBow Press rev. date: 12/19/2017

Trust in the Lord with all your heart
And do not lean on your own understanding.
In all your ways acknowledge Him
And He will make your paths straight.
—Proverbs 3:5–6 (NASB)

This book is dedicated to my three children,
Scott Egan, Ame Verduzco, and Betsy Sarconi.

CONTENTS

ACKNOWLEDGMENTS

I wrote this book for my grandchildren—in order of birth, they are Christopher, Taylor Mary, Drake, Madison, Jacob, Samantha, Megan, Danielle, Natalie, Mary Jane, Camryn, Emily, and Avry—and my great-grandson, Jonah, so they will have peace and purpose in their lives.

Marina Hibdon Hubbard and Bryan Hibdon, I am enjoying the opportunity to journey through life with you as your stepmom.

Rachel Oliveira, thank you for never giving up on me and praying for this book to be finished and published.

Jonathan Verduzco, Gavin Sarconi, and Mike Hubbard, thank you for loving and caring for our children and grandchildren.

Maryjane Choate, a.k.a. Mother, thanks for believing I would eventually get it right, and for all the laughter and giggles we've shared.

Cynthia, Jayne, Debbie, Joan, Bill, and Steve: There are no words to express the depth of my love for you or the sadness and regret I feel about the inconsiderate acts I have committed against you and your families throughout our lifetime as siblings. Let us rejoice that this book acknowledges what love and forgiveness can do in our lives.

Betsy Anderson, Peggy Harder, Charlyn Hulsman, Pam Basinger, Vicki Hanger, Marilyn Jakovich, and Joan Whitley: Thank you for your steadfast friendship through thick and thin. You listen, pray, and reason with me about how to get through situations, or at least get the most out of them, no matter where I find myself. What joy you bring to my Christian life.

Scot Montroy, Jennifer Olson, Jenny O'Hara, and Glenda Penic: Thank you for being such an enjoyable part of my life.

I have saved the best for last. Michael, my husband, friend, and fellow adventurer, thank you for our Christian walks together. It has been an incredible journey of love to get to this mountain top with you.

INTRODUCTION

I wrote this book for sons and daughters who are going away to college or leaving home for another reason. I hope that the insight expressed here will ease the transition and hopefully ensure it is better than expected.

The Holy Spirit informed my heart that peace and purpose come from intimate knowledge of our Father in heaven, Jesus Christ, and the Holy Spirit. On May 8, 2007, I knew I would finish this book and that after I completed the chapters and verses, I would write something about the Holy Spirit. The computer started doing annoying things, as it often did while I was writing this book, so I moved to a comfortable seat and started praying: "In the name of Jesus, get behind me Satan." I glanced over and there was Charles Spurgeon's book *Morning and Evening* sitting on the table. I picked it up and thought, *I haven't read tonight's reading,* and low and behold, as God would have it, here is what it said:

The Plurality of God
"Now acquaint yourself with Him and be at peace." Job 22:21 (NKJV)

If we want to acquaint ourselves with God and be at peace, we need to know Him as He is revealed in scripture. We must know Him not only in the unity of His essence and substance, but also in the plurality of His persons. God said, "Let us make man in our image" (Genesis 1:26 NASB). Let you and I not be content until we know something about that "us."

Endeavor to know the Father. Bury your head in His neck with deep repentance. Confess that you are not worthy to be called His child. Receive the kiss of His Love. Let the token of His eternal faithfulness be a ring on your finger. Sit at His table and let you heart be merry in His grace.

Also seek to know the Son of God, who is the brightness of His Father's glory. The Son, with unspeakable condescension of grace, became man for our sakes. Know Him in the singular complexity of His nature, for He is both eternal God and suffering finite man.

Do not forget the Holy Spirit. Obtain an understanding of His nature, character, attributes, and works. Look at the Spirit of God; he "was hovering over the face of the waters" (Genesis 1:2 NKJV), and brought order from chaos. This same Spirit now visits the chaos of your soul and creates the order of holiness.

An intelligent, scriptural, and experimental belief in the Trinity-in-Unity is yours if you truly know God and this knowledge brings peace.

—Charles Spurgeon, *Morning and Evening*, reading for May 8, 20007

Trust in the Lord with all your heart
And do not lean on your own understanding.
In all your ways acknowledge Him,
And He will make your paths straight.
—Proverbs 3:5–6 (NASB)

More ancient manuscripts in Greek and Latin documenting that the Bible is true have survived than manuscripts discussing any other subject from that time. Archeologists are still proving that the Bible is correct, and the text in the Dead Sea Scrolls matches the Bibles we use today.

God created us, knows us, and loves us. It only makes sense then to listen to His instructions and try to do what He says. It is like an owner's manual for a car. If you obey God's instructions, you will "run right" and find His kind of power to live. If you ignore them, you will have breakdowns, accidents, and engine failures. (Do not confuse this with the incidents He purposes for our growth and closer walk with Him.)

This book is a trust and faith journey with God, Jesus, and the Holy Spirit (wisdom, a.k.a. the small, still voice). We have a choice: we can live in our own realm or live in God's realm, where we cannot see Him, yet we can experience Him and His love for us.

A great way to experience God is to pray.

> My heavenly Father,
>
> Holy is your name. I am a sinner and I need your help. Please forgive me for the sins that I have committed in thought, word and deed.

Please remember—nothing is hidden from God, so recite in your mind all those sins that you need Him to forgive. There are no sins He will not forgive. Next ask Him to help you to forgive those persons who have harmed you in any way. Remember that if God is to forgive us, then we need to forgive others—even our enemies. If this is hard for you, ask for God for His help and strength.

Now name the people and things for which you are thankful:

_____

_____

_____

_____

> Dear Lord,
>
> Please open my heart and mind to what *your plans* are for my life. These are the things I love to do and you have given me these talents.

Now, list your talents:

_____

_____

Now tell Him your dreams. Talk to Him as if he already knows every hair on your head. He created you, and you are wonderfully made. You are His beloved child, so go for it! God can also handle hearing what you are hurt or angry about, so this is a good time for that too. Tell Him:

> I need your guidance and direction as I go through this manual. Please enlighten me about where you want me to be. Help me to be receptive to your will for me, just for today. That still, small voice is a mystery to me; however, I would like to acknowledge it today and maybe do what it says, just to test this new possibility in my life. [Look at the clock, and be still and quiet for eight to ten minutes; wait and listen for that small still voice.]

> Bless me and increase my territory. Protect me from the evil one so that I will have no pain and cause no one any pain. [This is from the Prayer of Jabez.]

> Thank you for being my helper in all that I will embark upon.

> In Jesus's name, I pray. Amen.

Growing into a life with peace and purpose means that each time we pray, we talk, and then we listen to the Holy Spirit. We cannot have a relationship with our heavenly Father if we never listen. Try not to fight or ignore the small still voice, because if you do, you will always wish you had not!

The Blessing of Obedience
Our Lord never insists upon obedience:
He tell us very emphatically what we ought to do,
But he never takes means to make us do it.
We have to obey Him out of a oneness of spirit …

The Lord does not give me rules,
He makes His standards very clear,
And if my relationship to Him is that of love,
I will do what He says without any hesitation.
If I hesitate,
It is because I love someone else in competition with Him,
Namely, myself.
Jesus Christ will not help me to obey Him,
I must obey Him; and when I do obey Him,

I fulfill my spiritual destiny.

My personal life may be crowded with small petty incidents,

Altogether unnoticeable and mean;

But if I obey Jesus Christ in the haphazard circumstances,

They become pinholes, through which I see the face of God,

And when I stand face to face with God

I will discover that through my obedience

Thousands were blessed.

When once God's redemption comes to the point of obedience

In a human soul, it always creates.

If I obey Jesus Christ,

The redemption of God will rush through me to other lives,

Because behind the deed of obedience

Is the reality of Almighty God.

—Oswald Chambers, *My Utmost Devotional Bible*, reading 45

CHAPTER 1
COUNTDOWN

Preserve me, O God, for I take refuge in You.
I said to the Lord, "You are my Lord;
I have no good besides you."
—Psalm 16:1–2 (NASB)

What a time for mixed emotions. Suddenly it is happening, the moment you have been waiting for and dreaming about: You are leaving home. You are going to be on your own. So why doesn't it feel better? It is okay to feel anxious, scared, and happy all at the same time. The trouble is that your parents or stepparents are no doubt acting peculiar. They are happy for you one minute, lecturing another, and downright weird another.

Think about what is happening. Your parents love you and aren't really sure they have taught you well or strengthened you for what you are about to embark upon. They also realize that they can't imagine what it will be like without you around. Loving and letting go gets real weird right about now. Needy parents will make it easy for you to stay, and healthy parents will help you to leave.

You will start to notice, more and more, what you don't like about each parent. This is your own individuality coming out. However, this is the time to remind your parents about the things you have learned from them that will help you make mature decisions when you are on your own. This is the time to acknowledge that differences of opinions are okay and that this is not a win-lose battle. Honoring individuality is gracious and ends up as a win-win for everyone.

Growing in your own direction is healthy, but it is also okay to say aloud, and often, that you will miss your family. Our heavenly Father created us to need and love one another. Tell your family what you will miss about them, and make no mention about what you will *not* miss.

Your parents have invested a lot of time and energy in you. They have gone to work to provide a roof over your head, food for your health, a bed to sleep in, and clothes for your body. Some parents will be angry, because they now wish they had spent more time with you. When anger pops up, it usually means the person is sad, hurt, or afraid. Don't let this emotion ruin the precious time you have together. Ask the angry person, "what are you sad about?" or "why do you feel hurt?" or "what are you afraid of?" And then *listen*.

Your Parents' Investment

One to three years dealing with you crying with no regard for time of day; giving you baths; changing dirty, smelly diapers; feeding you (and warming bottles—not too hot or too cold); dressing and undressing you; cleaning up sticky, spilled drinks or food off of the floor; watching you roll over, crawl, walk, run, skip, hop, and ride a bicycle; and teaching you how to talk (hopefully, appropriately).

Then there's the next eighteen years, with you getting bumps and scratches on your body (big and small, while their hearts skip beats); dealing with tears, tantrums, laughing, and crying; getting you to school on time; making you do chores and homework and compete in sports (wins and losses, hugs, kisses, studying, not studying, and getting all kinds of grades). And there's punishment, shopping, buying clothes and shoes, finding lost items (usually with no patience on your part), preparing meals for you (approximately 16,200 of them), washing your clothes (approximately 1,950 loads), getting stains out of your favorite outfit, folding your clothes, taking you places, arguing a point of view, dealing with you talking back, and most important, spending seventeen or eighteen years living with you and watching you while you were busy living your life.

Please have some compassion and grace and mercy for these people. They have loved you and have been very close to you, and now you are leaving. Who knows whom you will meet? Your parents will not have much control, which is very scary to them. You are an important part of their lives, no matter what it may feel like from your side.

Everyone's fear goes away when you communicate. It doesn't matter who admits it first; the main thing is to admit it. And if some people don't admit it, shame on them. You and your family may be afraid that there won't be enough money to help you out, or that they won't be able to say no when appropriate (and when it's the best thing for you, whether you want to hear it or not). Show them your budget, which chapter 7 will help you prepare, and this way they will see how responsible you are.

Keep an open mind when you go through this manual with them. They will make suggestions about what you have written, and this is the time to honor their thoughts. Think about what they are suggesting, because they, more than anyone else, know you and your spending habits as well as your other habits. Money is a big concern for your family. What you say and do can reassure them you are mature and ready to be on your own. Yes, you may have to bite the bullet and listen and ponder.

> A wise son [or daughter] accepts his [her] father's discipline,
> But a scoffer does not listen to rebuke.
> From the fruit of a man's mouth he enjoys good,
> But the desire of the treacherous is violence.
> The one who guards his mouth preserves his life;
> The one who opens wide his lips comes to ruin.
> The soul of the sluggard craves and gets nothing,
> But the soul of the diligent is made fat.
> The righteous man hates falsehood,
> But a wicked man acts disgustingly and shamefully.
> Righteousness guards the one whose way is blameless,
> But wickedness subverts the sinner.
> —Proverbs 13:1–6 (NASB)

> Poverty and shame will come to him who neglects discipline,
> But he who regards reproof will be honored.
> —Proverbs 3:18 (NASB)

When an opinion is given, the best response may be a simple oh, followed by your repetition of what was just said. In this way,

1. You are validating them.
2. They realize you really were listening to them.
3. Somehow, it causes you to be more objective about what they just said.

This valuable tool works with parents, siblings, friends, and coworkers. Afterward, count to seven slowly, and don't react. Move on to another topic, or say, "I'll have to think about that."

If your parents do not do some of the things you want to do, you might have some hidden resentment. Talk to them, using compassion and humility. Let them tell you what it was like for them when they left home.

Ages Eighteen to Twenty-Eight Are the Discovery Years: Why Rush?

This is the time to settle into yourself and take the opportunity to find out what you like and dislike, form your own opinions, and learn how to love yourself and love God. When we take the time to get into a right relationship with the Lord, He will be allowed to pour out His love to us. And it is then that the mate He has created just for you will come forth.

Statistics prove that people who wait until they are twenty-eight or older to get married drastically reduce the risk of divorce. Their marriages are happier and stay intact.

Right now is a very good time to dream. While reading this book, lots of ideas will come and go. The years after you leave home should be an adventure and a time when you can learn about yourself and the world.

Advice: Part 1

- Explore you feelings, emotions, and thoughts.
- Change your mind; nothing is set in concrete.
- Travel anywhere you want, anywhere you can afford.
- Try different jobs to find out what you love to do.
- Go to college; take any classes you want.
- Participate in any sport you want to try.
- Get into thought-provoking conversations.
- Stay up all night or as late as you want.
- Change your style—clothes, hair, makeup, etc. You can do it two or three times (or more)!
- Join different groups and clubs.
- Check out the opera, go to the theater, and discuss movies.
- Date, and date and date!

Advice: Part 2

- Do leave home with your parents' blessings.
- Don't leave home because of an argument or without a plan.
- Don't get married just because it will take you away from a small town, an awful family, a poor family, or a terrible neighborhood.
- Leave home prepared and with a vision.
- Dreams come true when God's will is done. He prepares your way.

Jesus Teaches Us Not to Worry.

In the book of Matthew, Jesus teaches us not to worry. Jesus, the Son of God, takes His time while addressing this problem. He says to trust His Father with the details of your life. Be in the now so that your efforts won't be hampered by concern about the future. That is not helpful. When you worry and fret, you aren't relying on His outcome; you want your own outcome. Worrying keeps you from God's will for your life. Live one day at a time, so that worry won't consume you.

> Therefore, I tell you, do not worry about your life, what you will eat or drink: or about your body, what you will wear. Is not life more than food, and the body more than clothes? Look at the birds of the air: they do not sow or reap or store away in barns and yet your heavenly Father feeds them. Are you not much more valuable than they? Can anyone of you by worrying add a single hour to your life? And why do you worry about clothes? See how the flowers of the field grow. They do not labor or spin. Yet I tell you not even Solomon in all his splendor was dressed like one of these. If that is how God clothes the grass of the field, which is here today and tomorrow is thrown into the fire, will he not much more clothe you—you of little faith? So do not worry, saying, "What shall we eat?" or "What shall we drink?" or "What shall we wear?" For the pagans run after all these things, and your heavenly Father knows that you need them. But seek first His kingdom and His righteousness, and all these things will be given to you as well. Therefore, do not worry about tomorrow, for tomorrow will worry about itself. Each day has enough trouble of its own.
> —Matthew 6:25–34 (NABRE)

The Armor of God
Be strong in the Lord and in His mighty power.

Put on the full armor of God,
So that you can stand against the schemes of the evil one.

Gird yourself with the
belt of truth.
God's truth defeats Satan's lies.

Put on the
breastplate of righteousness.
You will protect your heart with God's righteousness
when Satan attacks this area of your being.
(Your heart is the seat of your emotions, self-worth, and trust.)

Put on the
footgear of readiness to spread the gospel.
God gives you the motivation to continue to proclaim the true
peace that is available through Jesus Christ's death on the cross
when Satan wants you to think that telling others
about the good news is a worthless and hopeless task.

Hold tight to the
shield of faith!
God's perspective of any situation is your victory if you step out in
faith believing that the ultimate victory is yours. Having faith
shields and protects you against the flaming arrows of Satan.

Put on the
helmet of salvation.
The helmet protects your mind from doubting God's saving grace.
Satan wants you to doubt God, Jesus, and your salvation.

Wield the
sword of the spirit!
God's Word teaches you to take the offensive against Satan when
you are tempted. Fervently praying in all situations with all kinds
of prayers and requests allows God to use you in any circumstances
to do His will.

(from Ephesians 6:10-17)

CHAPTER 2
A VISION / A PLAN

It is extremely difficult to put a jigsaw puzzle together without first seeing the picture it will become. So it is with your life. You cannot make something out of your life if you do not have an image of how it should look.

A Vision for the Future

The next two pages are blank. Draw a picture or pictures of what you want your life to look like in the future. Draw pictures of what you want to do. Draw pictures of what you want to have. Draw pictures of what you want to do for others. Examples might include a cap and gown, college, nice home, car, family, clothes, washer and dryer, a vacation, to name a few. If you do not like to draw, cut pictures from magazines or write something down. God is awesome and huge, so think big and get to know yourself by determining what you love to do. This is your vision.

The Bible states:

> When people do not accept divine guidance, they run wild. But whoever obeys the law is joyful.
> —Proverbs 29:18 (NLT)

> If people can't see what God is doing, they stumble all over themselves; but when they attend to what He reveals they are most blessed.
> —Proverbs 29:18 (MSG)

Think about the video of your life they'll play at your funeral!

> Hope deferred makes the heart sick, but desire fulfilled is a tree of life.
> —Proverbs 13:12 (NASB)

Life Is about Choices and Consequences

When you have a picture of what you want to become, it will help determine your choices. When we obey God and our parents, He blesses us, and when we disobey there are consequences.

Your picture will be damaged if you break the law, become addicted (to drinking, drugs, gambling, etc.), get pregnant, or get someone pregnant.

If you choose to have sexual intercourse, you will probably get pregnant or get someone pregnant (with or without protection). There is no foolproof method against pregnancy except abstinence. God created sexual intercourse for consummating marriage vows of commitment, not for another type of relationship because of the delayed grief, emotional pain, or children. It is great for the moment; however, God wants a whole lot more for you and wants to spare you this grief and pain. You are His beloved child, and he does not want you to settle for less than you deserve.

Think about the people you know who have broken the law, are addicts, or had a child out of wedlock. What are they going through emotionally and financially?

1. What is happening to Person A because of his/her choices?

2. What is happening to Person B because of his or her choices?

3. What is happening to Person C because of his or her choices?

4. What is happening to Person D because of his or her choices?

If any of these possibilities exist in your life, and this exercise is too hard for you to do, ask God for His strength and protection. Do not put yourself in a place where any of these choices rule. Run! And don't go back for your hat!

The better your picture, the better your boundaries will be, and the better the chance you will end up with a great mate. Your kids will thank you for taking the time to pick their other parent.

If you choose stubbornness, procrastination, alcohol, drugs, or gambling, there will be a period when you feel invincible, but this will be followed by a roller coaster ride that may end in jail or prison or poverty or a breakdown.

Obsessive behavior ruins:

- families
- friendships
- marriages
- college
- careers

Addictions can kill the following:

- you
- innocent children
- innocent fathers and mothers
- innocent people

Choose life so that you may live it abundantly; then you will leave a legacy of which you can be proud.

Accomplishing Your Goal

Write down the steps you'll need to take to accomplish your goal. Below, there are lines with dollar signs and lines for time. Determine how much it will cost to achieve your goal and how much time it will take. Be reasonable about length of time, but don't let it scare you. If either cost or schedule seems unattainable, break them down into parts that are manageable. If you do not know the cost or how long it will take, ask someone who has accomplished this goal. Get more than one opinion.

There will be detours, setbacks, and interruptions. However, just like the jigsaw puzzle, in time, with faith, patience, and hope, it will be completed.

I want to become a _____.

I can do these jobs right now to learn more about this occupation:

Schools Known for This Career	Cost Per Year	Years to Finish
Junior Colleges		
	$	
	$	
	$	
Four-year Colleges		
	$	
	$	
	$	
Trade schools		
	$	
	$	
	$	

Notes

Circle characteristics you would like to have.

- righteousness
- humility
- fearful of God
- blameless
- loving
- meek
- prudent
- sincere
- undefiled
- watchful
- patient
- gracious
- discernment
- bold
- merciful
- attentive to the Holy Spirit
- harmless
- lowly
- obedient
- pure in heart
- steadfast
- upright
- joyful
- calm
- wisdom

> A good name is to be more desired than great wealth,
> Favor is better than silver and gold. (Proverbs 22:1 NASB)

Pray to God and ask Him to change your heart regarding any of the areas with which you need help.

Which of my habits or characteristics will help me achieve the goal in my picture?

1.

2.

3.

4.

5.

6.

7.

8.

Which habits or characteristics do I need to change?

1.

2.

3.

4.

5.

6.

7.

8.

Ask someone who knows you well for constructive critiques about both lists.

What is my ten-year plan? (Write down things you want to save for and own—car, travel, home etc.).

1.

2.

3.

4.

5.

6.

7.

8.

9.

10.

The Vision of Time

5	10	15	20	25	30	35	40	45	50	55	60	65	70	75	80	85	90

Circle your age on this timeline. Notice how many years you have ahead of you and how many are behind you. Put a square around your parents' ages. For most people, life brings more wisdom the more years they live.

Your Christian walk is a journey through time, places, and relationships with multiple changes. Look at the years ahead of you, thoughtfully with prayer; this will help you to look beyond today. You will see there is enough time to pray and search for God's will and vision for your heart and mind's desires to come to fruition. God does not set you in concrete. He loves change.

The vision of time helps you to decide when to venture beyond the places where you live, work or play, if you think that is God's plan for you. Do your homework with

God by meditating, praying, and listening to the Holy Spirit impart His wisdom to you; then you can pave the way for change. Rushing into change can be viewed as lazy because if God's plans for you are to succeed, you have to do your homework. Proverbs 15:22 (NASB) says, "The way of the lazy is as a hedge of thorns, but the path of the upright is a highway," which means that if you make changes without taking the time to plan, you'll encounter many rough spots. Whether you decide to move on or to wait can mean the difference between thorns or a highway. "Cease striving and know that I am God" (Psalm 46:10 NASB). God loves you so much that He is working out all the details. He is weeding out the thorns for you.

Psalm 46:10 says, "Without consultation plans are frustrated, but with many counselors they succeed," which means when you seek advice from people you trust, remind them that your conversations are confidential. Listen and weigh what they have to say. Wait with peace so that your family and friends can see your faith and trust in the Lord. Faith in the heavenly Father, Jesus, and the Holy Spirit protects you from the darts of the devil: "… [take] up the shield of faith, with which you will be able to extinguish all the flaming arrows of the evil one" (Ephesians 6:16 NASB). As the Bible says, faith extinguishes all of the devil's flaming arrows. The wait is unbelievably worth it. God's timing is awesome because so many things will fall into place and without much hassle. You may doubt God, but He does not mind being tested.

The vision of time helps to put your human relationships in perspective. Over time, your relationships will bring you love, joy, monotony, drudgery, trouble, or pain. A personal relationship with the heavenly Father, Jesus, and the Holy Spirit is the one relationship you can always count on. Knowing them changes your other relationships. You can no longer do and say whatever you feel like. Contemplation sets in. You know you are a sinner. When you sin, you ask for forgiveness. In all situations, large or small, you go immediately to the Lord and pray, asking Him to change hearts. If there is anything you feel unable to do, you can ask the Lord for a change of heart and His strength to do it. Wait, and see what happens.

Looking ahead to the years to come presents a bigger picture; thus, waiting until you're in your late twenties or thirties to marry doesn't seem like such a long time. You want to be sure you have chosen wisely. Look at all those years that lie ahead of you! Going to college now, while you are single, means that when you do have a family, you will have a better job, a higher income from a job you love to do, and more time to be with those you love.

Hopefully, you will be drawn to a personal relationship with our heavenly Father, Jesus, and the Holy Spirit. If so, you will experience a depth of peace and purpose that will make your life healthy and filled with joy even through suffering, troubles, and trials.

It is never too late to give time to your heavenly Father, Jesus, and the Holy Spirit.

CHAPTER 3
PONDER AND PRAY

Rejoice always, pray without ceasing,
in everything give thanks;
for this is God's will
for you in Christ Jesus.
—1 Thessalonians 5:16–18 (NASB)

Dear heavenly Father,

Please open my heart and mind so that I will come to know and do what your will is for me. Help me surrender my will so that I may have peace, purpose, and joy in my life.

Father, I am just beginning on my journey, and there is so much I think I know, and there is so much to learn. Help me to remember that my sin separates us and that I must ask for your forgiveness when I sin in thought, word, or deed. I am a sinner. I ask for your strength. I am weak. Help me ask my parents, stepparents, brothers, and sisters for their forgiveness when I trespass against them. Help me honor my parents. I ask now for your strength to help me forgive those who have hurt or harmed me in any way because, as you say in Ephesians 4:32 (NASB), "Be kind to one another, tender-hearted, forgiving each other, just as God in Christ also has forgiven you."

Help me put my trust in you, oh Lord, and not in people. Help me have the faith I need for this journey.

Please surround me with Christ-minded people who will remind me that your grace is sufficient. Holy Spirit, please help me to hear your small still voice in all that I do and act upon your wisdom rather than argue the point.

Be with my family and friends as I move out of my home, as I move out on my own. Give them the peace that passes all understanding. Help them to see me as a capable person, who is making the right move. Help me assure them that I am not going alone because you are going with me.

Thank you for your promise in Hebrews 13:5 (NASB). You told me that if I keep my life free from the love of money and be content with what you give me, "I will never desert you, nor will I ever forsake you."

Thank you for being my helper in all that I will embark upon. Thank you for sending your Son to die for my sins and leaving the Holy Spirit to impart your wisdom.

Lord, I close now with the prayer of Jabez so that I too may be honorable. "Oh that you would bless me indeed and enlarge my border, and that your hand might be with me, and that you would keep me from harm that it may not pain me!" (1 Chronicles 4:10 NASB). God granted Jabez what he had requested.

In Jesus's name I pray. Amen.

> So, as those who have been chosen by God,
> Holy and beloved,
> Put on a heart of
> Compassion,
> Kindness,
> Humility,
> Gentleness
> and
> Patience.
> —Colossians 3:12 (NASB)

A Typical Day as God Would Have It

It was going to be a very busy day. I had a lot to do, so I knew my daily Bible study was a must. I sat down, and got out my devotional Bible and read the lesson marked with the yellow ribbon. When I was through, I talked to the Lord very quietly in my head and heart. I asked Him to help me accomplish His will. He already knew what I hoped to accomplish; however, I wanted His wisdom in all that I was about. I also prayed, "Dear Lord, please let me obey your small still voice. Please do not let me argue the Holy Spirit's wisdom in all that I am to get done, and please don't let me forget anything. And please give me travel mercies (watch over me and keep me safe from harm while I travel)!"

This was my to-do list:

1. Grocery shopping for the boat. Six of us were going on the Newport-to-Ensenada Race (starting the next day) and, of course, time to put the provisions away.
2. Pick up Charlyn and Keith at the Burbank Airport at 2:30 p.m. (We lived in San Pedro, at least one hour away in good traffic.)
3. Go to the bakery I like in Torrance and get macaroons for our friends Mark and Stephanie.

I sat and meditated. I was very quiet, waiting to hear that small still voice.

The small still voice said, "Get going. Get the groceries and then put them away." Having learned to have faith in that small still voice, I got it done. However, I was watching the clock, and I knew how long it would take me to put the groceries. I knew I wouldn't have time to get to the bakery and also pick up my friends on time. I prayed about what to do next, and again the Holy Spirit said, "Get to Burbank." Back in the car I got and sailed down the 110 to the 5, getting to Burbank Airport with no delays. As I approached the city, with forty minutes to spare, the Holy Spirit said, "Bakery in Burbank." Well, I laughed out loud and told the Lord He had a great sense of humor, that I loved Him and His wonderful wisdom. I knew the area well because of work I had done in the area many years ago, so I parked the car and walked to the first bakery I saw down the street. I was surprised to learn that they did not make macaroons. I said, "Okay, God, you have another plan that will be revealed."

I looked for another bakery. By this time, I had to go to the bathroom, and a Fuddruckers came into view; I knew that would be a good place to use the bathroom. While there, I saw a cell phone on the toilet paper container. I talked to God in my head and heart and said, *I don't have time to turn this in.* (Oh, yes, I argued with the Holy Spirit). Then I thought, *What if someone else comes in and they don't turn it in? Okay, God, I do know the right thing to do.* I walked to the counter with the phone, and the lady said, "The manager is right over there." As I turned toward the manager, I noticed that the Fuddruckers had a bakery, and guess what the baker was taking out of the oven? Yup, freshly baked macaroons! Oh, boy, now I felt happy and silly. I bought the best macaroons.

God loved me so much that he not only helped me do what I needed to do, He also returned that phone to its rightful owner, and so I got to do something for Him. He knew I loved this journey of ours because I was praying each day to be surrendered to His will for me. After many years of waiting on the Lord, it was such a joy to watch how He pulled things off, so much better than I would have. (There was that moment when I said, *I don't want to do this, yet thy will be done, not mine.*) Once more I was glad I had faith in what He would accomplish in my life. I didn't waste any emotions getting upset, and by remaining calm I was able to greet my friends at the airport with joy and a great story to share. It gave me such joy to say to Charlyn and Keith, "God loves you so much He got me here without traffic and on time," and to Mark and Stephanie, "God loves you so much He made sure you would have freshly baked macaroons."

Be still, and know that He is God.

God's order often looks haphazard. We plan and fret, trying to work things out for ourselves or for others. We can't know all the facts, so things go wrong. If we surrender our will to God, we'll find His order will come to us, even if haphazardly. If a person does not know God, that person depends entirely on his own wisdom and forecasting. When we trust God's wisdom and concentrate on His plan for us, we meet and see Him, our Father, watching out for our well-being. The plan comes together much more smoothly and calmly and usually filled with joy! Our heavenly Father loves ordinary and haphazard. He loves to surprise us with a phone call, a text, a change of weather, a card, or a new plan for our life. He is so into us, individually.

Jesus was about His Father's will. What an example God gave us.

CHAPTER 4

CHOOSING WHERE TO LIVE

I lift up my eyes to the mountains,
from where shall my help come?
My help comes from the Lord,
who made heaven and earth,
He will not allow your foot to slip;
He who keeps you will not slumber.
Behold, he who keeps Israel
will neither slumber nor sleep.

The Lord is your keeper;
The Lord is your shade on your right hand.
The sun will not smite you by day,
nor the moon by night.

The Lord will protect you from all evil
He will keep your soul.
The Lord will guard your going out
and your coming in
from this time forth and forever.
— Psalm 121 (NASB)

Have faith that since He knows every hair on your head and everything about you, He will guide you to just the right town and place to live. Pray for wisdom in each decision you will make. Jesus is sitting right next to you and wants you to tell

Him about everything that is in your heart and mind. This chapter may help you determine your direction and hopefully enlighten you. Listen to that small still voice, if it is kind and loving.

Think about your past, and know that the good things you love to do are usually in line with God's plan. Pray for the Lord to reveal your true feelings and thoughts as you move through this process.

Climate Considerations

The fact that we have four seasons does not mean that each season lasts three months. Winter can last six months in some places. Humidity can make the summer feel very long. Lots of rain and overcast weather cause depression in some people.

The following chart will help you determine which region is best for you.

On a scale of 1–10, from worst to best, indicate what type of climate and weather-related activities you desire. For each item, consider, *How do I honestly feel about this?*

	1	2	3	4	5	6	7	8	9	10
City										
Country										
Slow Pace										
Fast Pace										
Sunny										
Lots of Rain										
Little Rain										
Cold										
Arid										
Hot										
Humid										
Snow										
Shoveling Snow										
Skiing										
Water skiing										
Hunting or fishing										
Swimming										

Prepare plans by consultation.
—Proverbs 20:18 (NASB)

If older students, friends, or acquaintances attend a school or live where you might want to go, when they return home to the neighborhood, invite them for coffee. (You should pay for the coffee.) Tell them that you want to better acquaint yourself with the school or area where they live. Take a notebook and write down their answers to the questions below. Once they understand your motives, they probably will tell you things that will help you make a final choice. Use the same notebook for each interview, so it is easy to review the pros and cons of each place. After three interviews, you might get confused.

If you go to a college in another state, remember there is an additional fee for out-of-state students. Find out how much it is up front. This could be costly, so think about what you are getting yourself into (e.g., fewer visits home).

If you want to stay in the same state but have a limited income, enroll in a city or junior college in the town of your choice. Many banks, fast food businesses, and organizations offer scholarships to students who work or volunteer for them. Work or volunteer for a business or an organization that is willing to work with your school schedule.

Call, e-mail, or write the chambers of commerce in the cities or towns where you want to move. Ask them to send you a packet of information about the city or town. Ask them to send you a local newspaper, or go online to get a feel for the area. Newspaper ads will inform you about available jobs and housing costs.

If possible, plan a trip with some or all your family members to each of the places on your list. Everyone on this trip will make comments, which may or may not be useful. Don't jump to conclusions; this is the time to consider what you should do. (It also is a great way to show younger siblings what is out there.)

Moving will be your biggest out-of-pocket expense; that is why it will help to consider all these things. Multiple choices may give you more freedom to choose just the right place. There will be fewer surprises and disappointments. More positive things in your life means less resentment about your choices. You will feel better and allow yourself to enjoy your life. When a person is stuck with a bad decision he or she has made, the anger and sadness spread to whoever is around and causes further bad feelings.

Poor planning on my part should not create any bad drama for those around me.

Questions to Ask About Schools and Towns

You can find out about all of the following topics on the Internet; however, talking with someone who lives there will probably paint a more realistic picture.

Weather

1. How long does winter last?
2. How much rain do you get a year?
3. Does it rain all year long? Is there flooding?
4. Do thunderstorms keep you up at night?
5. How much is your heating bill per month?
6. How many months do you pay this?
7. How many months of snow do you get a year? How deep is it?
8. What are the high and low temperatures during winter?
9. Who clears the driveways, sidewalks, etc., where you live?
10. Is there fog there? How long does it last?
11. How long are the summer months?
12. What are the high and low temperatures during summer?
13. Is this an area with high humidity?
14. Which months are the most humid?

Work

1. Are there many jobs available for students with my skills?
2. Are there any big malls within walking distance from your apartment or school? *(Big malls mean job opportunities.)*
3. Is there seasonal work?
4. What large corporations are in the area?
5. What is the pay scale? *(If the rent is cheap, your income probably will be less than you expect and vice versa.)*

Transportation

1. Are there municipal buses? Do they run on a decent schedule?
2. Are there subway/train stations within walking distance?
3. Where is the closest airport?
4. Can I get around without too much bother without a car?

Entertainment

1. Are there bowling alleys?
2. Movie theaters?
3. Parks?
4. Ocean?
5. Lakes?
6. Rivers?
7. Mountains?
8. Skating or roller rinks?
9. Amusement parks?
10. Swimming pools?
11. YMCA or YWCA?
12. Camp grounds?
13. College activities?

Hospitals

1. How many?
2. How far away?
3. Is there a medical facility on campus?
4. Does the school offer health insurance? What does it cost?

Churches

1. Churches with Bible study?
2. How far away?
3. Churches with a college pastor?
4. Churches with Saturday evening services?
5. Churches with a healthy college group?

Crime Rate

1. Are the police visible?
2. Where is the police station?
3. Which neighborhoods or areas are not safe?
4. Have you looked on the Internet to find out the crime rate?
5. How does the area rank nationwide.

Schools

    1. How many city colleges, state colleges, or universities are in the area?

Libraries

    1. How many libraries are there?
    2. Are they in convenient locations?

Places to Shop

    1. What shops are close by?

Post Office

    1. Is it in a convenient location?
    2. What alternatives are available?

General Questions

    1. What do you like most about this place?
    2. What do you dislike about this place?
    3. Compared to your hometown, do you think the cost of living is higher or lower?
    4. Why do you think that?

Determining Cost of Living: A Quick Checklist

- wages in the area
- rent (low rent usually means lower wages or not-so-nice areas, making safety an issue)
- car registration
- heating bill
- air conditioning
- car insurance
- groceries
- cold weather clothes (more expensive)
- costs of eating out
- car maintenance (cars wear out faster where salt is used on snow-covered highways)

CHAPTER 5
A PLACE TO LIVE

Behold, I am going to send an angel before you
to guard you along the way and
to bring you into the place which I have prepared.
—Exodus 23:20 (NASB)

Now you have picked out the school and town. Next, you must decide where to live. Pray, talk to God, and listen. That small still voice will give you amazing ideas.

As a Christian, you may find it helpful to talk to your pastor, depending on the size of your church. Ask him or her about a church affiliation in the area where you are moving. The pastor may put you in touch with someone seeking a roommate or a parishioner who now lives in your future home, and may help you find a comfortable place for yourself.

Pray, talk to God and listen.

Dorms

Dorms are good places to meet new people. Here are some things to consider:

- You may not get to choose your roommate.
- Alcohol, sex, and drugs abound in coed dorms.
- In coed dorms, your roommate may sleep with someone else in his or her bed and make it uncomfortable for you to stay there.
- Too much socializing may mean you have to study at the library.

- Your roommate may use your possessions, such as your computer, which could cause problems.
- You may need to set up boundaries to ensure a peaceful existence.

Are you strong enough to get through all of the above?

Dorm Food

Dorms offer different meal plans; if possible, ask someone when the best food is served. This plan is paid for when you register for school so think on this:

- Monday–Friday plans are great if you are not around on the weekends.
- If you don't eat breakfast, get the lunch and dinner plan.
- If you spend your money on clothes and fun, get a plan that includes weekends.
- If you are on a budget, get the Monday–Friday plan, and save your food throughout the week.

Colleges usually have bulletin boards listing rooms or apartments for rent or to share.

Apartments

Get on the Internet, look at online newspapers, check out available places to rent. Remember you will need the first and last month's rent or a deposit (depending on the housing laws in that area). Set up times to visit places that sound like they are what you want and where you want to be. It is best if you can visit a month or two weeks before you need the place, so you have plenty of time to check out at least five or six places. This will help you make a decent decision about where you will live.

Drive around the town to figure out the best location; try to find a place close to work and school). Keep in mind, if you do not have a job yet, consider the big picture; get a map and work out the distances to and from downtown (where jobs usually are). Consider driving in rush-hour traffic. Locate bus stops and get bus schedules as a travel backup.

Some things to ponder:

- The bigger the apartment, the larger the heating and air conditioning bills.
- The more roommates you have, the less privacy you'll have, but there will be more talking, more socializing, and more problems dealing with different personalities.

- Look at apartments in different price ranges and neighborhoods. Look during the day, and then go back at night to see what happens after dark.

Parking

Thinking about parking is a must if you have a car. Check out the parking availability during the day and at night to find out if parking is a problem; visiting in daytime won't give you a good picture because people will be at school and work. Your own carport, space, or garage is a must, especially in a well-populated area where you need to ensure a parking place. Without a designated space, you can waste a lot of time searching for parking, not to mention the walk from the car to home. Don't settle and think that you can always find a parking place.

- Many campuses and surrounding areas have restricted parking.
- Watch out for street-sweeping signs; tickets are costly and add up quickly.
- College and beach apartment complexes with poor parking facilities are notorious for:
  o People parking their cars behind yours, preventing you from getting your car out to go to class, or to work, or on a date.
  o Dents of all sizes on cars.
  o Residents wasting an hour or more trying to find parking places.
  o Parking tickets, because residents became so frustrated they park illegally. An alternative is a bicycle; keep it in your room, have a good anti-theft device, and register the bike with the police.

Apartment Managers

An important part of deciding where to live asking questions of apartment managers, e.g.:

- How far are we from public transportation? (This is good to know in case your car breaks down.)
- How far are we from the market or mall?
- How much do utilities cost?
- Are utilities included in the rent?
- Do nearby trains, planes, or freeways cause too much noise?
- Check out the actual apartment you will be renting, not a model or someone else's apartment that's "just like" the one you'll be getting.

If you see the place at night, try to see it in the daylight as well. As always, the least amount of time on the highway equals more sleep time, although it never seems to add up to more study time. If you can't find what you really want, get a month-to-month place; do not sign a long-term lease. Remember this first place will not be yours forever, but it will give you some time to get used to where you are.

This is very important: Read the contract. Ask questions. Before you move in, write down everything that is wrong, broken, or missing in the apartment. There should be a place in the contract for these items. If the owner or manager is upset because you are documenting the problems down, tries to intimidate you, or says he or she "will take care of it," be persistent. Get a date for completion of the repairs.

Designate a notebook or notepad just for notes about your apartment. Take notes and date them. If you end up in small claims court, your notes will be admissible evidence. If someone does not want to rent to you because of your concerns, go somewhere else, or drop your complaints and take lots of pictures before you move in, so that when you move out the landlord cannot blame you for the damages and deduct the costs from your security deposit. It is better to have solid evidence like photographs when you take the landlord to court to get your money back or if he or she sues you. If you use your cell phone to take notes and photographs, be sure to back them up. Phones can get stolen, lost, or broken.

You will be charged the first month's rent plus a security deposit or, in some places, first and last month's rent plus a security deposit. Pets are likely to increase security deposit. In all cases, you will have to fight to get that security deposit back. Here are some guidelines to go by:

Apartment Checklist

1.	Screens missing?	Bent	Torn	Room
	Screens missing?	Bent	Torn	Room
	Screens missing?	Bent	Torn	Room
	Screens missing?	Bent	Torn	Room
	Screens missing?	Bent	Torn	Room

2. Holes in walls or ceilings? Check behind doors; door handles can put holes in walls when doorstops are missing. List the rooms that are damaged.

3. Carpet stains? List each and every one in all the rooms.

4. Problems in the kitchen?
   o Handles missing?
   o Stove clean?
   o How many racks present?
   o Stove missing any knobs? Are all burners working?
   o Refrigerator clean? Are racks missing?
   o Floor under refrigerator damaged?
   o Dishwasher working? Racks present and working?
   o Cabinet doors okay?
   o Does the sink drain quickly?
   o Knicks in the porcelain sink?
   o Garbage disposal present and working?
   o How old are the appliances? Are they all in good working order?

5. Condition of floors, both linoleum and hard wood?

6. Tile chipped?

7. Closet doors on tracks?

8. Sliding doors on tracks?

9. Draperies clean, torn, or stained?

10. Patio?

11. Faucets?

12. Bathrooms?
   o tubs
   o shower
   o sinks
   o toilet

13. Plants—alive or dead?

14. Other problems?

No matter how nice owners or managers are when they take your money, when you move out, you will pay for all damages that are not on your list. Keep a copy of this list, and take care of the place. Keep a file folder for recording the details of your new life.

If you move in with someone who has been there for a while, do the same thing. Make a list, and give copies to your roommate and the landlord; put the original in your file. If your roommate moves out first, you could pay for any damages he or she causes.

Read the contract the roommate filled out. If he or she cannot find it, ask the landlord for a copy. Make sure both roommate and landlord understand you will only pay for damages you incur.

Always make your rent check payable to the apartment owner. Paying in cash to a roommate is always very risky because if he/she gets into a jam and uses the cash for something else or decides to skip out and leave you alone, you are out that money. If you ever give cash to the landlord, make sure you get a receipt. Keep all receipts in your file folder.

When you leave an apartment, take pictures of it when it is empty. One roll of film or a disposable camera can save you $50 to $1,000-plus in a security deposit. Judges in small claims court love to see pictures. Depending on the situation, the pictures may reduce the amount of money you owe or allow you to get your entire security deposit back. Take pictures of damage you caused, so there is a factual document, and the damage won't be blown out of proportion by the owner or landlord. Remember that judges prefer to rule on actual photographs and your phone might be lost, stolen, or not charged when you need the evidence.

There are many nice landlords; however, you probably do not have a history with yours. It is better to be safe than sorry.

CHAPTER 6

WHAT TO TAKE

The Armor of God

Starting from the top as you dress for the day …

Put on your head the

helmet of salvation.

The helmet protects your mind from doubting God's saving grace.

Satan wants you to doubt God, Jesus and our salvation.

Put on your

breastplate of righteousness.

God's righteousness protects your heart

when Satan attacks this area of your being.

[This is the seat of your emotions, self-worth, and trust.]

Put on your

belt of truth.

God's truth defeats Satan's lies.

Put on your shoes which are the

footgear of readiness to spread the gospel.

God gives you the motivation to continue to proclaim the true

peace that is available through Jesus Christ's death on the cross

when Satan wants you to think that telling others

about the good news is a worthless and hopeless task.

Hold tight to the

shield of faith.

God's perspective of any situation is your victory if you step out in

faith believing that the ultimate victory is yours. Having faith
shields and protects you against the flaming arrows of Satan.
Wield the
sword of the spirit.
God's word teaches you to take the offensive against Satan when
you are tempted. Fervently praying in all situations with all kinds
of prayers and requests allows God to use you in any circumstances
to do His will.

This is my interpretation of Ephesians 6:10–17 (NASB).

The first thing you must have is a file folder (see below), preferably a plastic one with the handle, so you can keep all your important papers together—social security papers, rental agreement, bills, and bank statements, etc. If you can lock it, all the better.

Clothes

Wait until you get where you are going to buy clothes because styles in your new town may be slightly different than where you live now. The basic clothes you have will be fine, and you can accessorize after you have settled down.

Warning

The things you leave behind may or may not be considered sacred to your family members who are still at home. Pack up whatever is still valuable to you, and mark it with a large note: *Do not discard! Property of [Your Name]! Important to me!*

There's a chance your parents will want to clear out your old room, or a sister or brother will want to make more room for their stuff. Do not think that the safe place where you stored your things in the past will remain safe after you leave. Mark and use duct tape to seal your boxes, and put them in an attic, basement, or garage—preferably a hard-to-get-to place.

Your siblings may wear the clothes you leave behind, no matter what you discussed with them. Once you are out of sight, they'll think, "She won't mind."

The Essentials

If you can't afford a car, don't worry. A lot of students ride bicycles or take the bus. Transportation will be the least of your worries if you have read the previous chapters. More often than not, you will meet up with someone who has a car, and you can always give them money for gas.

Rather than buying lots of items, consider taking whatever essential things you already have and waiting to get anything else until you see what your roommate has. It is nice to have matching bedspreads, so if you must shop, buy towels and sheets in neutral colors, like tan or white, so things won't clash. (These also all can be washed in the same load; see chapter 11.). You will probably move at the start of each year while you are in college, and neutral things will go with any décor, and you will have more money for fun.

Before you buy anything, call home and ask your parents if they have anything you can use for your place; they may have what you need in the garage or attic, and you can get it on a trip home. Don't be bashful about locating the Goodwill store or second-hand stores; you can save money shopping in such places. For the best deals, go to second-hand stores near wealthy neighborhoods. Check clothes for stains, and try them on. Take your time, and look for quality name brands you can trust.

What to Put in Your File Folder

Purchase a box of manila folders. Colored ones make for more pleasant filing!

Label one for each month. Every time you get a receipt for a purchase, put it in the folder for that month. At the end of the month, go back and see how you spent your money. You will be glad you did this if you need to return something for an exchange or because it was defective. It is also a way to track what you've paid for cash.

Additional Labels

- birth certificate
- social security papers/card
- Department of Motor Vehicles (DMV) documents, e.g., tickets, driver's education certificate, traffic school verification
- copies of car insurance and registration papers (keep originals in the car)
- car maintenance records

- medical insurance documents
- rental agreement
- warranties and equipment manuals
- employment papers

CHAPTER 7
BUDGET

God's Advice about Money

The book of Proverbs offers practical instruction about the use of money, although sometimes it is advice we'd rather not hear. It's more comfortable to continue in our habits than to learn how to use money more wisely.

Be Cautious
A man lacking in sense pledges and becomes guarantor in the presence of his neighbor. (Proverbs 17:18 NASB)

Do not be among those who give pledges, among those who become guarantor for debts. If you have nothing with which to pay, why should he take your bed from under you? (Proverbs 22:26–27 NASB)

Don't Accept Bribes
A wicked man receives a bribe from the bosom to pervert the ways of justice. (Proverbs 17:23 NASB)

Help the Poor
One who is gracious to a poor man lends to the Lord, and He will repay him for his good deed. (Proverbs 19:17 NASB)

Be Careful About Borrowing:
The rich rules over the poor, and the borrower becomes the lender's slave. Proverbs 22:7 (NASB)

Give Tithes to the Church

"Bring the whole tithe into the storehouse, so that there may be food in my house, and test me now in this," says the Lord of Hosts, "if I will not open for you the windows of heaven and pour out for you a blessing until it overflows." (Malachi 3:10 NASB)

Budgeting takes practice and persistence. The biggest problems that arise are unplanned expenses, such as the car breaking down, or an unplanned trip, or you find something at a great price, etc. To be successful, a budget must be carried out. It makes sense to look at a budget as money to be spent instead of money you can't spend.

Handling Monthly Bills

As discussed in a previous chapter, you'll need either first and last month's rent as a deposit on a new apartment or first month's rent plus a security deposit; usually there is an additional charge for pets. You can keep track of your other expenses—both monthly and weekly—on a checklist, such as the one below. Use a pencil (easy to erase) to keep track.

Monthly Bills

Rent _____

Utilities:
- o   water
- o   gas
- o   electric
- o   garbage _____

Phone _____

Internet _____

Car payment _____
- o   insurance
- o   registration   (Divide by twelve, and save that amount each month.)
- o   oil change   (Every 3,000 miles.)
- o   repairs   (Timing depends on age of the car.)
- o   parking fees
- o   traffic tickets _____

Medical bills   _____

Clothes and shoes   _____

Tithing. It is important for godly people to give 10 percent of their incomes to the church. I challenge you to do this because God honors us when we return to Him what was His from the start. This is all about honoring our Creator and living according to His will. It is amazing how much further your money goes when you tithe. Please test this concept, and then step back and watch what happens!

Weekly Bills

Tithes to the church   _____

Food   _____

Personal hygiene   _____

Laundry   _____

Gasoline   _____

Entertainment/eating out   _____

Miscellaneous (stamps, paper, books, etc.) _____

Total   _____

Wages

Find out what your living expenses will be first, so you can determine what kind of job and wages you will need. Often people find out after they have taken a job that the salary doesn't cover their expenses; then they go to the boss as if it is his or her fault because they are not paid enough. The reality is that they didn't do their homework. Going into an interview with an idea of what you need to cover your expenses gives you a starting point, and you won't come out short every month and slowly go into debt. An alternative is to get two part-time jobs or a part-time job in addition to your full-time work. Pray, listen, and trust in Him to guide you to a job that will pay the bills.

Use this formula to calculate your monthly income:

$____ per hour × ____ hours per week × ____ days worked/month = $____ gross monthly income

Subtract taxes (go to bankrate.com to calculate your taxes).

If you are paid on a weekly basis, figure out how much will go toward your bills. Say 95 percent of your total income goes to monthly bills; then each week you may spend 5 percent on whatever.

Get counsel from the person who hired you or the finance department to find out what your take-home pay will be, but never disclose your salary to a coworker.

School Tuition

Determine what you'll pay for schools on a yearly basis. Tuition can range from $200/unit to $1,000/unit, and books can cost $200 to $500 each quarter or semester.

Have a regular checking account and then get two saving accounts—one for school expenses and the other for car expenses.

Utilities

Apartment managers are a useful source of information about the costs of utilities. Climate or weather can play a big part in the cost, so always ask about the average yearly costs for air conditioning in the summer or heating in the winter. Make allowances for seasonal bills.

Phone Bills

If you get behind in your phone bill, always pay something, and it won't be disconnected. Don't be overwhelmed by the amount; pay a little extra each month to pay it off. The debt will show up on your credit score, etc. To save money, use e-mail or send postcards and letters. Don't leave your cell phone around; it might be borrowed or stolen. There are lots of options for phones. Choose one that fits your budget, not someone else's!

Cash or Check?

Don't pay bills with cash, especially the rent; it gives roommates too much of a temptation and often leads to heartache. Many people have gotten stung by paying their share of the rent in cash to a roommate, who takes off with the cash. Write a check to the person or company listed on the apartment contract, which gives you a record that you have paid. The other alternative is to go to the post office (usually less expensive than a bank) and buy a money order; again, you'll have a record.

Banking

Always balance your checkbook. Pick a day a week to go over your addition and subtraction in your checkbook. Always get a receipt from the ATM when you withdraw cash or make a deposit. When you get back into the car, make it a habit to write what you have just paid for in your checkbook and put the receipt in your wallet or checkbook. These moments will save you a great deal of aggravation and money and prevent the likelihood of being overdrawn. Every time you are overdrawn, the bank will charge $10 to $30 or more. Think about what you could do with that money.

Check your bank statements. It is not hard to do if you pray first and ask for the Holy Spirit's wisdom. The bank statement is the truth and reminds you about what you forgot to put in your checkbook as well as any bank fees incurred over the month. Checking it helps ensure your records match the bank's. A bank teller or manager can show you how to reconcile your statement and checkbook if you have never done this before. The first time is free; however, you will be charged in the future. Mini statements are great, and the $1–$2 fee is cheap in terms of peace of mind.

Online banking is a wonderful way to check your account; no matter which method you use, you must take time to do this!

Try to put 1 percent of each paycheck in a savings account for your future, and don't touch it, no matter what.

Stick to Your Budget

Never be embarrassed about sticking to your budget. If someone makes fun of you, shame on him or her. It is easier to say, "I'm sorry, I can't do that; it isn't in my budget" than to say, "I can't afford it" or "I don't have the money." People think differently about you when they know you are careful with your money. They respect you.

If you love to read magazines, go to the library, where they're free, the selection is incredible, and it's quiet.

If you love to watch movies, go to the library, and borrow a DVD. It's free.

Find enjoyment in things that don't cost money.

CHAPTER 8
ROOMMATES

Behold, how good and how pleasant it is
for brothers (who know the Lord)
to dwell together in unity!
—Psalm 133:1 (NASB)

Roommates are not perfect, but neither are you. You will learn about boundaries—theirs and yours. You will learn about tolerance, what you can and cannot stand. It can be an emotionally interesting time because you are walking into the unknown. Listen and observe.

If you can interview roommates, here is some helpful advice:

- Visit them unexpectedly. Try not to be shocked if you are surprised by what you see. And remember—what you see is likely what you will get.
- Ask them about a variety of subjects. Discuss your thoughts on each subject. Use your notebook or the outline below.

Name_____

Phone number_____

Address _____

_____

Subjects to Discuss

- What kind of music do you like?
- Do you listen to music while you study?
- How many hours per day do you spend watching TV or videos?
- How many hours per day do you spend playing video games?
- Do you have your own computer, or do you use the ones at the library or your roommate's? (Roommates have been known to "borrow" their roommate's computer without permission, so this information can be helpful with up front boundaries about your computer.)
- Are you on the computer a lot? The answer to this question will inform you about the type of person you will be sharing a living space with.
- Do you do your homework first or do you put it off until the last minute?
- How are the household bills divided up and paid?
- What chores do you like to do?
- What chores do you hate to do?
- What are your good habits?
- What are your unpleasant habits?

Look Around the Apartment

Are their surroundings:

- comfortable   yes   no
- extremely neat   yes   no
- livable   yes   no
- organized   yes   no
- recently vacuumed   yes   no

Get yourself a drink of water and see if

- the kitchen is okay   yes   no
- there are pets (especially if you have allergies)   yes   no
- the litter box is clean   yes   no
- current roommate likes living there   yes   no
- the bathroom is clean   yes   no

Write down any additional things you notice.

After you have interviewed your intended roommate, invite his or her current roommate for coffee and a chat. Here are some potential questions to ask:

- Chores are a pain. How do you manage?
- What is studying like?
- How often do you all party?
- Are there any challenges with paying the bills?
- Does everyone share everything, or are things considered pretty sacred?

These other people will give insight into your future roommate's lifestyle. Listen to how they answer every question. Rely too on your own observations. Just because people appear a certain way does not mean they live how they look.

Try to find out good points and bad points—yours and the roommate's—ahead of time. Things mentioned up front are easy to accept because they are out in the open.

- Can I cope and live with this person?
- I cannot change anyone but myself!

Consider whether this person likes to be alone or joins in with the group. Let him or her know your thoughts and feelings as well.

When a person becomes your roommate, sooner or later, the two of you will get into an argument—probably about something that annoys one of you. If the issue had been aired ahead of time, then there will be no depth to the argument, because it was always out in the open.

We cannot change the wind, but we can adjust our sails. Once I had a roommate who waited until a couple of days before a project was due and then drove me crazy as she rushed to complete the assignment. Somehow, she always got an A. But I thought she should plan ahead and do a little at a time, until I realized that was how she was, so I no longer got caught up in the craziness. I went to the library and stayed out of her way. We compromised; she moved her projects to the kitchen table or living room, and I got a restful night's sleep. Communication is key. *Poor planning on your part does not create an emergency on my part.*

Keep a perspective about what you want so you can achieve your objectives. Listen to how your roommate talks about money, i.e., borrowing it, repaying it, overdue bills, work ethic, etc. Ponder, pray, and ask God to reveal anything you have not discerned.

Think about the whole person; if each person has ten issues, can you live with your roommate's ten issues? Can your roommate live with yours?

It is easier if your roommates are on the same economical scale as you are. If you are barely getting by and you have a roommate whose parents pay for everything, that can be very hard on the relationship. It is best to have these dear friends live with someone else and keep them as dear friends.

If your study habits are poor, it is helpful to get a roommate who studies more than you do. Set yourself up to complete school. Set yourself up to win!

I finally had to remove the temptation of going out on school nights by going to the library as soon after dinner as possible—before anyone mentioned pinochle or a movie or a party. My reward for studying in the library was to party hearty Friday and Saturday nights and sleep late on the weekends. I did the laundry whenever, and other chores had to be done by Sunday at 8 p.m.

Discipline is hard, but it got me through four years of college. Roommates without discipline can derail your plans. It is important to stay focused; write down your goals so people cannot get you off your course. Remember your vision.

Roommates may or may not want to do things with you; it in no way means they like or dislike you or are mad at you. Do not force them to do what you want to do; go and find someone else or go by yourself (as long as it's safe). Do not let them force you to doing something you don't have time for either.

CHAPTER 9
COMMUNICATION

A wicked messenger falls into adversity,
but a faithful envoy brings healing.
— Proverbs 13:17 (NASB)

Communication Takes Practice

It will help your relationship if you can talk to other people. Repeat back what someone says to you, and see how good you are at listening and communicating. Did you really hear what he or she said, and did the other person really say what was meant.

Ask for more information. Some people don't give you enough information to complete a job correctly and then get upset with you when it isn't done the way they wanted. Beware! People with the best intentions can set you up for failure. You cannot read minds, and no one can read your mind. Go over the information you have been given, and fill in any areas of doubt by asking, "I need more information about _____."

Always discuss situations, clarifications, or problems by starting:

- I think
- I feel
- I hate it when this happens

Never use:

- You said
- You did
- I hate it when you
- You always
- You never

The truth is often something like this: "On Saturday I felt bad when Sue came over, and I wasn't included in the conversation."

But what usually gets said is this: "Whenever Sue comes over, you never include me in the conversation."

A response to the first statement might have been "I am sorry, I didn't know you wanted to be a part of the conversation with Sue on Saturday."

But because the second statement is what is usually said, often the response is "You always act like you don't want Sue to come over."

Remember that you can be as hard to live with as the other person is.

1. List specific details about the issue. "I feel _____ when _____ happens. Can we talk about this?"

2. Give a reason why something is bothering you. "This _____ bothers me because _____."

3. Work with the other person. "What kind of a solution can we come up with?"

If both of you follow these guidelines, you will understand each other better and see that both of you may contribute to problems. I cannot tell you how many times problems disappear when we have all the pieces to the puzzle. It is also very healthy to give other people the opportunity to share their hurts and problems.

There are troubled people or people who become irresponsible due to misfortune or drugs. Do not hesitate to help them seek help. Do *not* become their caretaker. At this time in your life, keeping your mind and heart focused on your education will lead to successes and healthier failures in your future. Having your mind and heart set on fixing and changing others leads to destructive behavior and attitudes—yours and theirs. If you find yourself in the above situation, look for help on the Internet, ask a school counselor for help, or check out the pamphlets in the counselors' office. Call the counseling center at your church. Attend open twelve-step meetings in the community. You can lead a horse to water but you can't make it drink! Al-A-Non- is for family and friends of the addict (it is a twelve-step program to prevent enabling).

Always work on yourself, not on other people. Change only comes from within.

When you feel you have helped as much as you can, then remove yourself form the situation, or you will be brought down too.

Remaining healthy is essential to the completion of your education, holding a job, earning a promotion, and starting a career. Being a healthy person brings success, peace, and purpose.

Distancing yourself from problem people is healthy and wise, and we all need to set boundaries. Where alcohol and drugs (recreational or prescription) abound, trouble of the worst kind will eventually rear its ugly head.

Honor One Another

Do not try to change anyone. We can only change ourselves. Take care of yourself. People who are struggling will suck you in to their problems, and get you off your path and vision. No matter how strong you are, you cannot save them. They have to take action for themselves. You can point out their addictive behavior and take them to counseling (colleges offer them for free) or twelve-step meetings. You can pray for them, show them Jabez's Prayer, and recite it with them.

A roommate, friend, girlfriend, or boyfriend who drinks alcohol or uses drugs everyday has a problem. Addictive, obsessive people who are not in counseling, therapy, or a twelve-step program are not healthy. Communication with these people gets you and them nowhere! Get out of these situations as fast as you can. If circumstances dictate, attend Al-A-Non meetings, so you can cope.

Remember—nothing is set in concrete. If things are not working out, agree to stay out of each other's way until a solution can be reached. Prayer now can just be for "a change of heart." Many solutions come with time and prayer.

Communicating by leaving and taking good messages can make life more pleasant. When you live with a roommate or roommates, being alone can be precious. Designate a notebook where you and your roommates can record time departed and estimated time of return. If you commit to doing this, it will free up time for a bubble bath with your favorite music and candles or a private phone call for at least ____ minutes. You also could set up blocks of time when each person can be alone; record those times in the book or ask for alone time at weekly intervals.

If you aren't coming home for a meal, call or leave a note. Buy a message book for phone calls, and then there will be two copies—one to take and one in case the first note gets lost. Never tear the copy out of the book; write the message on another piece of paper. Good records can prevent problems or a tough situation. Sometimes cell phones aren't charged or are broken, stolen, or lost, so this is a back-up plan.

This is an exciting time to start good habits that will be appreciated by others throughout your lifetime. Practice being considerate.

A spiral notebook or a phone message book ($10.00+ at an office supply store) is best for messages. It is big enough, it won't get lost, and past messages can be retrieved. It helps to date the message in case you ever need to remember when you last heard from someone. Always keep the book in the same place. You can always go to the same place, no matter who is home or what they are doing, and get all your messages.

Taking incomplete messages or forgetting to tell someone about a call can cause a lot of unnecessary hurt. Always repeat the message you have taken back to the caller (even if it's for yourself). Humans are not perfect. Don't let someone off the hook by not asking him or her to repeat the message you've given.

If you are consistent and insistent on taking good messages, people will think well of you, and that respect will carry into work and marriage.

Noise

If you have problems with noise of any kind, you can get ear plugs at the pharmacy or drug store. Foam plugs are the best; they fit any size ear canal and don't try to return to their original size while they're in your ear canal. They are reusable and can be washed with soap and water. They are also great for swimming, studying, and sleeping. The secret is to roll them down into the size of the lead in a pencil, pull back on your ear (women) or up or down on your ear (men), and insert the plug. It will expand to the contour of your ear; you will notice the difference. You have them in correctly if everything sounds monotone.

Moodiness

Watch out for pouting and jealousy when there are multiple roommates. It is okay to mention, "I am feeling left out. I would like to be included in your plans." Don't speculate about what someone else is thinking. Come right out and ask, "Okay, what is the matter? What is going on?" I am still surprised by how often this statement gets right to the crux of the problem.

CHAPTER 10
PROBLEM ROOMMATES

Keeping away from strife
is an honor for a man,
But any fool will quarrel.
—Proverbs 20:3 (NASB)

The first one to plead his case seems right,
until another comes and examines him.
—Proverbs 18:17 (NASB)

Do not say terrible things about the "problem person" or gather advice from everyone. Perhaps you do not have all the puzzle pieces, or you have been misinformed. The process that follows is intended to help all concerned avoid embarrassment.

Be truthful. When you are alone with the other person, talk about the issue; explain that there are things that are not right between you, are confusing to you, are really bothering you.

Acknowledge that the other person probably has grievances too, and ask when would be a good time to discuss both sides in private.

Do not have the conversation at that point, no matter what. Neither of you is prepared. To prepare, you need to pray over the situations. Preparation clarifies and doesn't allow for anger and mean things to be said and regretted later.

Sometimes we cause as many problems as the other person does. We must forgive others so that God can forgive us.

Working Through Problems Worksheet

Use this worksheet to guide your conversation. (Make copies for future use.)

It bothers me when you

Do you know you …

I like it when you

1.

2.

3.

4.

5.

Thank you for

I am sorry about

Dear Lord, thank You for helping us to work out our differences.

Reread chapter 9, "Communication." When situations are not healthy for either party, other living arrangements should be made as soon as is possible. Usually people have someone in their lives with whom they can stay, at least for two or three days until other arrangements can be made. Do not overstay, as then you will become the problem roommate. It is okay to find another place to live. Do not be hard on yourself; look at this as not so much as failure but as growth.

Suggestion: When you move in to a place, remember that situations change. You need to be flexible. It is wise to have an alternate plan in place just in case. This might mean reading the rentals in the newspaper from time to time, or checking out various neighborhoods to see what alternatives are available.

Dear God,

You know my situation, and I need Your help. You know every hair on my head, so help me to find a safe and affordable place to live. Help us in the move.

Amen.

CHAPTER 11
CHORES

Whatever your hand finds to do,
do it with all your might.
— Ecclesiastes 9:10 (NASB)

As the Lord's beloved sons and daughters, we can change any ordinary situation into something extraordinary. Whatever we are doing—chores, dishes, taking out the garbage, filing, or any menial task—ceases to become commonplace when we do it unto the Lord.

Adaptability is the power to make a suitable environment out of any circumstance in which you find yourself. God was with Joseph in the well, traveling as a slave in a caravan, in Potiphar's home, in prison, in all of Joseph's situations, and Joseph honored God by doing what was right and good. And the Lord honored Joseph by making him a prince and saving his family.

Chores

How can chores be fair? They can't! However, they can be managed so that everyone's needs—not necessarily wants—are met. Because of the wide variety of attitudes and upbringing, household chores have to be negotiated, managed, renegotiated, and re-managed.

Get a spiral notebook for writing down chore assignments, and call a meeting of all roommates. No one can be absent. Choose someone to write in the book. Set down rules or guidelines such as:

- No whining.
- A chore can only go _ days without being done. Then there is a $_____ fine, which goes in a jar and can be used for a dinner out or ordering pizza, etc.
- If you cook, do your own dishes.

Set guidelines in the book like:

- Move furniture every third time you vacuum.
- Use a toilet brush and clean the toilet often.
- Keep a spray cleaner in the bathroom, so you can clean after taking a bath or shower. Use a mirror cleaner too.

List all the chores in the notebook. Go through each room of the house or apartment. This will help everyone communicate thoughts about what is a responsibility of the group and what is each persons' responsibility.

Some people have never cleaned. If you have people like this as your roommates, show them how the chore is done, and watch them do it when it is their turn. Never do for people what they can do for themselves. Do not criticize the work; instead, give them helpful tips to make the job easier or go faster (and at the same time will show them which places were missed).

Have each person log his or her chore with name and date completed in the chore book. If someone isn't doing his or her share, this is where it will show up.

This logbook is great because when someone wants to know what you have done, you don't have to repeat the list of things you've done and the time it took. Tell the person to look in the logbook; it is all right there in black and white. The logbook prevents arguments. Yes, some people may say it is a pain, but they are usually the ones not doing the work! Accountability is a great lesson!

If you like a clean home, people will allow you to do all the work, and it will eventually catch up with you. You will explode in anger, and your roommates will think you have a problem because they thought you didn't mind cleaning up. No martyrs. Trading chores helps keep things balanced so that everyone is helping. If you like it cleaner and neater than others do (put that on your list of roommate requirements) try to remember that when you get your own place, you will have control.

Don't be a weenie and get stuck doing more than your share. If dishes become a problem, get paper plates or colored place sets so people have their own. If someone always leaves stuff around, get a basket or plastic clothesbasket, put everything in it, and then put it in the person's corner. This is a way to clean a room without letting the culprit off the hook, especially if you have company coming. If other people's clutter bugs you, try to train them to put their stuff in the basket themselves.

Bathrooms

- Get small baskets for all your stuff—in one color so you know what is yours.
- Get the toilet cleaner brush in the stand; it will be ready to use anytime!
- The black gunk is mold and can be taken off with bleach.
- Clean the bathroom right after someone has taken a bath or shower; the moisture loosens the dirt.
- If you don't want to wipe down smooth painted ceilings in bathrooms, because there are colored spots that will stain, then make sure the vent is on or a window is open when you bathe or shower. Otherwise expect to pay for a new paint job when you move out.
- Avoid plugged drains; wipe sinks, tubs, showers after each use to get the hair out. (A quick and convenient way to clean the drain is with toilet paper.)

Kitchen

- Use cheap paper plates, and get wicker or plastic plate holders; they are cheap and save time and bother. To clean wicker plate holders, soak and use a bristle brush; they will dry like new.
- To clean burned or caked-on pots and pans, boil water in them, and use a spatula to scrape the food off while the water is boiling.
- Don't use abrasive scrubbers on glass coffee pots. Use vinegar or salt and ice to clean them.
- When wine spills on a tablecloth, pour salt on the stain; it will absorb the wine (and the process is fun to watch).
- Clean the stovetop after each use or at least once a day. The longer food stays on, the harder it is to get off!

Vacuuming

- Move furniture every four to six weeks.

Chimneys

- To avoid having smoke in the room, open the damper when making a fire. There is always a handle to open the chimney damper. Take ashes out. Don't vacuum them; just use the shovel. Put an aluminum pan under the wood. Don't throw wrapping paper in the fireplace; the roof will catch on fire. Chimneys do have to be cleaned yearly.

General Cleaning

- Wear rubber gloves when cleaning to protect your nails and skin from harsh cleansers.
- Never mix chlorine bleach with a cleanser; the fumes are deadly
- Clean when it rains or snows, and go outside when the weather is nice.
- Monday is the best day of the week to clean because everyone is around on Sunday, and the house will stay cleaner longer. However, clean whenever needed and better yet whenever you feel like it or have the time for it.
- Lighten up on cleaning. There are so many things to learn and do; there will always be cleaning.
- Try to clean together, so you'll have more time for fun together.
- Sometimes (rarely) you find someone who likes the chores you don't like and vice versa.

Laundry

- Laundromats are friendly places. Take along a book or magazine. Don't try to study here; this is a chore. Don't double up here. If the washer smells funny, don't use it. Someone may have used it to wash work clothes.
- Unattended clothes may be stolen. Double check washers and dryers for socks and underwear. It works best for me to use washers and dryers that are next to each other.
- Single females should never go alone at night to a laundromat; that is inviting trouble. If you must go alone, go to one that is very busy.
- Keep soap and bleach, etc., in the car trunk to ensure you never forget them. Bleach is deadly when splatters; it turns colors white. Use paper towels to wipe

down washers before you use them so drops of bleach do not get on clothes. The best bleach is all-purpose.

- Put two or three laundry baskets in your room. Sort your clothes as you peel them off—dark colors, whites, and pastels or lights. If you do not have time to put clean clothes away, laundry baskets work as well as drawers. Short on carrying bags for clean clothes to the car? Turn a pillowcase inside out, and right side out when you're done.

Simple Sorting and Temperatures

- Water temperature. Darks: cold. Lights: warm. Whites: hot
- Your white clothes look dingy or gray, but the label says "no bleach." What do you have to lose? Try bleaching them in warm water; they usually come out whiter. To clean really gray kitchen towels, soak them in one cup of bleach and two gallons of water over night; then wash with regular whites.
- Read instructions on detergent and bleach containers. However, one cup—never more—is a good rule to follow. Never more!
- Check pockets for IDs—I washed my son's a couple of times, and he was not a happy camper—and tissues.
- Turn dark clothes inside out when washing and drying them, and the color won't fade so fast.
- Most laundromats have machines that make change for $1, $5, and $10 bills. Otherwise, get a roll of quarters at the grocery store. I keep a cheap fanny pack in the car with the detergent to hold all my change. It allows me to keep my hands free and I don't have to worry about someone stealing my purse.
- Watch out for dreaded mildew—black spots. They may be green before they turn black. Mildew develops when wet clothes are covered with other clothes or plastic. Dry wet clothes before mixing them with other dirty clothes; mildew also can spread to other clothes.
- Any stains will eventually come out unless they are dried in the dryer, which sets the stain. Wash it again. Spray stain removers work well.

CHAPTER 12
COOKING

Now *He* who supplies seed to the sower,
and bread for food,
will supply and multiply your seed for sowing
and
increase the harvest at your righteousness.
—2 Corinthians 9:10 (NASB)

Cooking can be a delight or a chore. Here are some suggestions.

Collect your family's favorite recipes, and take them with you when you leave. It is nice to have them autograph and date them. Put them in a binder or folder with pockets, so you are ready to add to your collection at any time. Recipes are also fun to go through on a rainy day.

People come from all types of backgrounds. You may be surprised to discover how tasty different foods can be. Being on your own allows you to experience new things, and cooking will probably be one of them.

If you have never cooked before, take an adult education class in your hometown before you leave or in your new community. You will learn to cook and meet new people.

Do not be hard on yourself; it takes a while to learn to get everything to the table hot at the same time. Heat the oven at 250 to 300 degrees to keep things warm if time gets away from you.

A tablecloth and place settings make any meal look special.

If you have friends living nearby, suggest that you all shop together at one of the big discount stores, and split both the food and the bill in half.

If you like to eat out, breakfast is the least expensive meal. Another option is to eat at home, and then go out for dessert or coffee.

Hate eating alone? Invite people over and ask them to bring something. Or arrange a progressive dinner, especially when funds are limited: have salad at one home, the main course at another, and dessert at a third. Have potlucks on a Friday, Saturday, or Sunday night. Meet at your house or in a park. People love to bring something and then there is less preparation time, a.k.a., work, and more time for a card game, etc. This also works well for birthday parties instead of presents.

Use paper and plastic whenever you feel like it.

Sometimes roommates burn food. If you cook for them, they will never learn to cook. Subconsciously, they may be sabotaging this "chore" so they can get out of it. Be patient with them; have them cook soup or make sandwiches. Always keep soup handy for a backup!

When shopping, remember a lot of recipes are on the backs of packages, so you have a built-in shopping list.

Start a spice shoebox. Spices are expensive. Buy the small size, one or two at a time, and accumulate them in the shoebox. When you move on, there will be no dispute over which spices are yours. I believe each cook should have his or her own box, because all the cooks I know have favorite spices.

If you really do not like to cook, find someone who will cook and clean up in exchange for a free meal. Discuss your budget with them, and you buy the groceries on their shopping list, so you'll know much things cost, and no one can "pull the wool over your eyes." If they end up doing the shopping, check the receipts and food, and always ask for your change back. Do not accept what you have not inspected.

CHAPTER 13
FINDING OUT ABOUT YOURSELF

But the helper, the Holy Spirit,
whom the Father will send in my name,
He will teach you all things,
and bring to your remembrance all that I said to you.

Just because you are grown,
doesn't mean that you can't keep growing
in all the other areas of your life.
John 14:26 (NASB)

It is okay to be unsure about whom you are and what you really want. However, you can take charge of your life and give yourself peace and purpose. Find a quiet place, and pray, meditate, and then listen so the Holy Spirit can give you God's plan or vision for your life. (Refer to "The Blessing of Obedience" in the Introduction.) Wait upon the Lord by keeping silent and quiet. Listening for that small still voice is like waiting for a car to pull up with a long-lost friend.

Write down what is revealed to you, and ponder and pray about it. If it is good, then it is from the Lord. If it is hurtful or harmful, it is from Satan. At that time, a very fervent prayer would be, "In the name and blood of Jesus, get behind me, Satan."

Do what you need to do to accomplish your plan or vision. Before God parted the Red Sea, Moses had to step into the water. Similarly, sometimes we must step out in faith and believe that what He has set out to accomplish in our life will happen.

To keep your spiritual life alive and well in your new surroundings, ask your hometown pastor to recommend a church in the new area. Take on the responsibility of finding a church to which you'll love to go. Make sure the new pastor preaches and teaches from the Holy Bible and that his or her criteria match your biblical principles. Check out the church's Bible studies, meet and talk with the college pastor, and visit the college group on more than one occasion. If you have never attended church and you like someone who does, ask to accompany him or her to a service. Ask what you should wear so you don't embarrass yourself. Pray about this, and allow God to lead you. Or use your phone to find a church; and call and ask questions. Have paper and pencil ready to take down times of services (using the message book ensures you'll have the information in the future). Saturday night services are usually more casual and upbeat.

Take classes you like or want to take, at least one a semester or quarter. Ask the Parks and Recreation Department to send you its catalog of classes because it offers fun classes at very reasonable rates. This is a wonderful place to meet people who share your interests.

Try sports you've never tried before. Rent equipment before you buy it. Bicycles can sit for years without any attention; tennis may be just a fad. Don't buy the most expensive equipment unless you are competing and can afford it. Average equipment works just fine when you play for fun and are just starting out. If you borrow someone's equipment and it breaks, work something out so there are no hard feelings. (Watch out if someone says it doesn't matter, because you may find out later that it did.)

Don't join a gym until you have checked out the weight rooms and facilities at the junior or city colleges in your area. Sometimes the cost of a class is far less than the monthly fees at a gym. The class also may encourage you to go back.

College and university music departments often have rooms where you can practice your instrument without driving your roommates crazy. Usually you must sign up to reserve a time.

If you get into a financial bind or have problems with just about anything, schools provide counselors (free of charge) who will help get you back on the right track. Remember that financial problems are your responsibility, and getting a job, or a second job, to get out of debt shows growth. Check in with a pastor or counselor before you decide to quit school, because there are many ways to rearrange one's life to accommodate an education. Persevering with your education now will make life so much more enjoyable later.

Take charge of your life. Don't just let it happen.

CHAPTER 14

GIRLFRIENDS AND BOYFRIENDS

For this is the will of God, your sanctification,

That is that you should abstain from sexual immorality,

That each of you know how to possess his own vessel

In sanctification and honor,

Not in lustful passion, like the Gentiles who do not know God,

And that no man transgress,

And defraud his brother in the matter,

Because the Lord is the avenger in all these things,

Just as we also told you before and solemnly warned you.

For God has not called us for the purpose of impurity

But in sanctification.

So, he who rejects this is not rejecting man, but the God

Who gives His Holy Spirit to you

… for you yourselves are taught by God to love one another;

For indeed you do so toward all the brethren …

But we urge you, brethren, to excel still more;

And to make it your ambition to lead a quiet life, to attend to your own business,

And work with your own hands, just as we commanded you,

So that you will behave properly toward outsiders,

And not be in any need.

—1 Thessalonians 4:3–12 (NASB)

A self-defense class is one of the best investments you can make at this stage of your life. An ounce of prevention is worth a pound of cure. There is safety in action and in numbers.

There are good boyfriends, girlfriends, and guests; okay boyfriends, girlfriends, and guests; and awful boyfriends, girlfriends, and guests. When you are first starting out, you don't know who these people are. Finances play a big part in deciding to allow people to visit, if you have roommates. Honesty plays an even bigger part.

Talk to your roommates ahead of time if you plan to have a friend visit. Or write it down in the message book; include the dates of the visit and the name of your friend. Ask for a time to talk this over. Sending a text is another option, if their phones are charged and working.

Before your guests arrive, write down what you'd like to do while they visit, what you can afford (extra food, activities cost etc.), what you cannot pay for, and what they'll need to pay for. Plan meals and activities, you can afford. Do not ever hide the fact you are on a budget. It is a very wise person who lives on what he or she makes. Send the plans to your friends in a text, e-mail, or letter; keep a copy for yourself so when they call back you'll know what they are talking about. Or call them, and go over the plans on the phone. Again, writing it all down makes for an easy conversation on the phone, or if a text comes back with their response, you can check it against your list.

As you can probably guess by now, the goal is to eliminate arguments or "no one told me" scenarios. Also, good preparation ensures you'll spend quality time together. Trivial things that are overlooked can be the molehills that turn into mountains. This is an appropriate time to ask a Christian friend to pray with you so that nothing will be overlooked—weather, health, travel mercies, conversations, money, etc.

Make sure you set up enough alone time with your guests, so that you don't get mad at your roommates for taking up all your time. That is your fault, not theirs. Be considerate of your roommates who have shared their home too. If your guests have caused an added expense, show your appreciation by cooking a special meal for your roommates.

Don't have any expectations about the visit; let the time together happen. Be flexible, and consider the weather. Have alternate plans. This is a valuable time to see the friend in the real light. If something annoys you; you can't change him or her! If the visit doesn't go well, you are probably growing apart. Recognize it for what it is, and let it go. High-school reunions are an appropriate time to see if you still have something in common and to see if there is any reason to continue contact.

Regarding regular everyday visits from friends, it is healthy to set boundaries for yourself, e.g.,

I like it when this happens:

I do not like it when this happens:

Communicate, communicate, communicate.

You do not want to be a parent before you are ready. Meet at the library or go to the park; spend a lot of time in public places to get to know each other. Get creative about your time together. Private places cause lust and passion to take over, and they are such strong emotions that rarely are your values or morals able to withstand them.

Every single lady I know who has gotten pregnant thought it wouldn't or couldn't happen to her, so please, if you have intercourse, make sure you protect yourself. AIDS and sexually transmitted diseases are alive and thriving. Sex is like playing with a loaded gun.

Know your surroundings; keep it very public when you go on a date with someone you do not know very well. Pour your own non-alcoholic or alcoholic drinks at a party. Be prepared with an answer so if someone does make a remark you come off as a wise person: "Oh, I'm a very particular drinker. My tastes are very refined." Also keep your drink with you always; if you put it down, and leave the area get another drink. Do not trust anyone with your drink.

CHAPTER 15

MANNERS AND GIFTS

Every good thing given
and every perfect gift is from above,
coming down from the Father of Lights,
with whom there is no variation
or shifting shadow.
—James 1:17 (NASB)

Humble and gracious manners will encourage people to think of you as a good person. Good manners offer an opportunity to show your servant's heart.

Opening a door for someone is a wonderful gesture. If a door opens inward, walk through and surprise people by holding it open. The gesture will put a smile on the sullenest face. Open a car door whenever you can. Guys, help a lady with her coat. Offer her a chair and sit down only after she has been seated. Stand when a lady joins you at the table. And walk on the car side of the sidewalk. Think of manners as random acts of kindness. Always ask if it is okay to sit next to someone whenever you are not in your own home.

Eating appropriately makes a difference. If you were not taught how to hold a fork or to chew with your mouth closed, now is the time to learn. (If you have had an injury that prevents you from holding utensils properly, mention it right away in a matter-of-fact way.) One of your friends or roommates will know how to eat correctly; ask the one who is kind, thoughtful, and gentle to help you. Perhaps you can establish a secret signal; for example, your friend might tap on the table with his pointer finger when you forget to hold your fork correctly. Practice. Practice. Practice.

Pay attention to how other people use utensils, and copy their actions. Determining which plate is the bread plate can be confusing; if you forget which one it is, wait for someone else to use his or hers. Other helpful hints: Fine restaurants provide sorbet (fruit-flavored ice) between entrees to help your taste buds adjust! Break your bread into two to four pieces with your hands before you butter it. Put butter from the butter dish on your bread plate or dinner plate; then take it off the plate to butter your bread. Do the same with jam and jelly, whether out of a jar or from a dish. Packets of butter or jam can go right on the bread.

If you work as a waiter or waitress, you will learn about tipping and about people too. Fifteen percent of the total is appropriate for breakfast and lunch. An effortless way to tip correctly is to round up the total before doing your calculations; for example, if the bill is $23.82, round up to $24. Ten percent of $24 is $2.40, and 5 percent is half of that amount: $2.40 + $1.20 = $3.60 or $4. At dinner the tip should be 20 percent; if the bill is $56.50, round up to $60. Twenty percent of $60.00 is $12: that is your tip. Don't under tip—that shows you are without class—unless, of course, the server is very bad. If the food is bad, talk to the manager calmly and send it back. If you aren't treated well, do not return to the place. The nicer you are, the more likely you are to get a better deal. Dining should be enjoyable and relaxing.

Thank You Notes and Sympathy Cards

Buy a packet of thank you notes at the dollar store or card shop, and keep stamps on hand. Keep them in a manila folder in the file box for easy access. Mail the cards or give them in person.

Whenever you feel lonely, go to a card shop and pick up some assorted cards to keep on hand. Do not forget about get well and sympathy cards. Everyone loves to receive mail, and getting a card often prompts the recipient to make a long-distance phone call to the sender.

Sympathy cards mean so much after a death. Signing your name is sufficient. Now that you are over eighteen and on your own, this is a very mature kindness. Attending funerals is also very important to those left behind. If you didn't know the deceased, go for the survivors you do know.

Gifts

When you are visiting friends, don't forget to bring your hosts a gift. You don't have to spend a great deal of money. For example, buying a woman a single flower is better than arriving with nothing at all. At a flower stand, a single flower can cost from 75 cents to $2. She will cherish you for taking the time to buy it. Grocery store bouquets are great at any time. Money should not be the issue. Moms, grandmothers, aunts, and girlfriends love to get flowers. If you are spending a weekend with friends, flowers are great ways to say thanks to your host. Host gifts for guys include decks of cards or paper plates, cups, or disposable utensils (if they are in an apartment). Even a six-pack is a thoughtful gift. Try not to arrive anywhere empty handed, and do not take home the leftovers from the food or drinks you brought. Transfer them to another bowl, and leave them for the host and hostess unless, of course, they insist you take them.

Don't charge your gifts unless you have the money to pay the bill. This really irks parents and real friends. Thoughtfulness counts, but irresponsibility does not.

A smart way to Christmas shop is to get a big box or basket with a lid (or a trunk), and start in January. When you see something on sale that you know someone would like, get it, put their name on it, and toss it in the box. By November you could have enough presents for everyone without putting a dent in your pocketbook. (This box is also a major source for presents throughout the year.) Or join a Christmas savings plan and have money taken out of your check every pay period. By December, you'll have enough money to buy presents.

If the people in your life already have everything, make a donation in their names to their favorite charity, and put the acknowledgement in a card with a note. If it is a Christmas gift, put the card on a branch of the tree.

Most guys like tools, socks, CDs, something for the car, a subscription to a magazine, a book. Or cook a special dinner for him or take him on a picnic. If you are really broke, clean his apartment when he is away. Sneak over, and leave a happy birthday or Christmas card. Do not get into any personal stuff; just clean the living room and kitchen. Going to the zoo or museums are great gifts. Stamps and stationery, movie theater tickets, and fast-food gift cards or, better yet, grocery store gift cards make wonderful presents.

A wonderful way to get what you want or need is to make a dream list of five to ten items, and give a different list to people who will be giving you presents. This way you won't know exactly what you'll be getting; however, you will get what you want and need. Don't think people can read your mind, or set them up to fail because they didn't get what you anticipated.

When amounts have been set, do not spend a whole lot more because that makes everyone else feel bad. Honor one another by not changing the gift-giving boundaries.

At Christmas or any holiday, don't feel left out. Call a church and find out the caroling schedule. Go to a convalescent home, and play some cards with the patients. Serve food at a shelter.

It is okay to let people know when your birthday is and invite friends over; if you don't want presents, ask people to bring a can of food for a homeless shelter or a local pantry. Have a potluck. Potlucks are great for Friday or Saturday nights, Sunday afternoons, a Super Bowl party, Thanksgiving, Easter, Fourth of July, Memorial Day, Labor Day—whenever! Do not be alone on your birthday or holidays. It is the pits.

A gift of alcohol can create a problem. Many people no longer drink. Honor them by not trying to push drinks into their hands. One drink could kill an alcoholic, or someone may come from a dysfunctional drinking family and choose not to drink.

Be considerate of people with diabetes, food allergies, or on a special diet.

Call and say thank you whenever someone spends money on you. Babysitting or taking friends' kids to a museum, zoo, or park is a great way to say thanks for their kindnesses to you. Just showing up with an apple pie can put a smile on people's faces.

> There is one who scatters,
> And yet increases more,
> And there is one who withholds what is justly due,
> And yet it results only in want.
> The generous man will be prosperous,
> And he who waters will himself be watered.
> —Proverbs 11:24–25 (NASB)

CHAPTER 16
OBEY THE LAW

Sing to him a new song:
Play skillfully with a shout of joy.
For the Word of the Lord is upright,
And all His work is done in faithfulness.
He loves righteousness and justice;
The earth is full of the loving kindness of the Lord.
—Psalms 33:3–5 (NASB)

Traffic Tickets

The unknown can make one procrastinate. However, getting a traffic ticket is not a situation where procrastination is appropriate. Pay the ticket as fast as you can. The sooner you get this done, the better you will feel. Accept responsibility for forgetting to notice the sign that said, "No parking between 8 a.m. and 10 a.m. on Thursdays due to street sweeping." Don't kick the curb; your foot will really hurt.

Tickets accumulate; the police have an incredible system and will find you eventually, especially when you least expect it. They will find you. The cost of tickets escalates with age. The court will allow you to make payments; however you must call, write (keep a copy of your letter in your DMV file), or go down to the station to tell them your plans.

If the tickets are for parking violations, the police may put a hideous clamp on your car tire, and you will not be able to move your car. Of course, this will happen on a day when you are going somewhere very important. It never happens the day after finals or when you are just going for a drive.

If the parking meter was broken, pay the fine (put the check in the envelope), and then go to the nearest police station and report the location of the meter. They will return your money if the meter is broken. Therefore, you need to keep good track of the time when you put money in the meter and also when you returned to your car.

When you are charged with a moving violation you can plead not guilty; if the officer does not show up, your case could be dismissed. If you choose to do this, call ahead and find out exactly where you should show up to pay the fine (you will be reimbursed if you win), and set a court date. Ask when the court opens and closes and when is the least busy time. Take a book to read while you stand in line. The court staff will go over everything with you and tell you when the hearing is.

Dress as nicely as you can for the court date. If the officer shows up, you still have the option to go to traffic school. If you truly believe that there are unusual circumstances or the ticket was unfair, then be prepared. Write everything down, so you won't forget anything, even if you are nervous. Get a display board, and diagram what happened. Show the streets (with their names) and sidewalks, lights, and signs. Draw an X or O to indicate where the cars were. Label everything, and be sure to note how fast you were going and the amount of time the traffic lights take to change from green to yellow to red. Go back to the scene, and do your homework. If the traffic light changed too soon, tell the judge. Keep a disposable camera in your car as a backup, and use it as well as your phone. Pictures are great evidence. Go back and photograph the area if you don't have a camera on you at the time. Weigh whether this time and energy is worth the cost of the fine and if you are up to going through with it. You will be nervous; however, judges are usually fair. Keep your copies of the outcome in you file.

If you decide to go to traffic school, keep the proof you went in the DMV file. If you get another ticket you will have a record when you last attended and that will let you know if you can attend traffic school again. Be aware that the time periods between attending traffic school sometimes change. When you keep good records that are easy to find in your file, you can look up when you last went to traffic school with no hassle.

If you get a DUI, show up to court in clean, unwrinkled clothes and clean shaven. Show up! Go to the Alcoholics Anonymous meetings, attend the county coroner's meeting at the morgue—do everything that the court requires. Work out a payment plan. Don't be late to any place you are required to be. If you need help, see a counselor at your school or a pastor. Inform your boss about what has happened; you may need to take a day off to go to court. Be honest and accountable; accept responsibility for your actions. Use designated drivers, or find out about the free services available for drinkers who need a ride home. Go online to find the number for twelve-step programs in your neighborhood.

If you forget to do something or to show up somewhere, go to the court as soon as you can and clear the matter up immediately. If officials must find you, the consequences are usually much worse. If something isn't clear or you have any questions, raise your hand, and wait for the judge to give you permission to speak. No question is too dumb. Judges usually appreciate them and are there to clear up any confusion you may have. If you get nervous or are extremely shy write it all down and read from the paper, or give the paper to the judge to read.

Small Claims Court

This is your best option for getting back money that is owed to you, e.g., deposit on a rental, an unpaid loan, or reimbursement for unfair treatment. The judges are very fair, and the truth will come out. There's a cost to file the paperwork, there may be a fee to have a marshal deliver the papers, and the case may take up a morning or afternoon, so please measure the value of the process. Is this worth your while? Is this a profitable endeavor?

If you are summoned to small claims court, be sure to show up. Go prepared to tell the truth, and write it down because it is important not to forget anything. If you have written evidence for the judge, he or she may leave the bench/courtroom to look it over and ponder the decision. Sometimes the dollar amount you owe may be lowered due to the evidence you present. Or you may be able to set up a payment plan based on your financial situation, not on what the other party thinks you should do. Many times, $20 a month will be fine.

In Proverbs, God states that He wants justice, not sacrifice.